# Boris the Dog

Boris was a typical dog.

He liked to chase birds, sticks and tennis balls.

He enjoyed long walks across muddy fields and naps curled up in the sunshine.

He loved gobbling down tasty treats and chewing old, worn-out slippers.

## Practice Questions

**a** **Find** and **copy** a word that shows that Boris was a normal dog.

_____

**b** What did Boris like to do in the sunshine?

_____

Boris had two floppy ears, a big wet nose, four fluffy paws and a glossy fur coat. But Boris had something extra too – he had two tails. He'd always had two tails, and Boris thought this was quite normal until the day he went to dog training.

**1** Which parts of Boris were fluffy?

_____

1 mark

**2** When did Boris realise that dogs don't normally have two tails?

_____

1 mark

# Key Stage One English

## Set A
## Reading

## Paper 1: Reading Prompt and Answer Booklet

| First name | |
| --- | --- |
| Middle name | |
| Last name | |

**Total marks**

Exam Set EHEP13

# Useful Words

dog training

trainer

poodle

Dalmatian

dog show

Boris was looking forward to his first training session. He got so excited that he found it difficult to walk.

Most dogs can cope with walking and wagging their tail at the same time, but Boris had two tails to deal with. When one tail swung to the left, the other swung to the right, and Boris couldn't keep his balance.

He wobbled like a big bowl of jelly.

**3** What happened when Boris was excited?

_____

1 mark

**4** Why did Boris find it difficult to keep his balance?

_____

1 mark

**5** Which word from the text tells you how Boris was moving? Tick **one** box.

walked ☐    swung ☐

wobbled ☐    bounced ☐

1 mark

Boris was the first to arrive at the training hall, so he sat inside, waiting for the others. He had managed to calm down. His tails had stopped wagging, and he was using them as a handy little cushion.

As the others arrived, they walked past Boris, giving him a welcoming sniff and a cheerful woof.

**6** Why couldn't the other dogs see Boris's two tails when they first arrived? Tick **one** box.

- They didn't notice Boris. ☐
- Boris had wrapped his tails in a scarf. ☐
- Boris was sitting on his tails. ☐
- Boris had his back against the wall. ☐

**7** **Find** and **copy** two words that show that the other dogs were friendly towards Boris.

1. _____

2. _____

The hall was full, and training could begin. "Boris, come to me. Good boy," called the trainer, who stood in the middle of the circle with all the dogs facing her. Boris leapt to his feet and did as he was told.

Gasps of surprise echoed around the room as the others saw Boris, and howls of laughter filled the air.

**8** How did Boris respond to the trainer? Tick **one** box.

☐ He ignored the trainer.
☐ He went up to the trainer.
☐ He jumped onto the trainer.
☐ He copied the trainer.

**9** What **two** sounds could be heard in the training hall after Boris leapt to his feet?

1. _____

2. _____

"He's got two tails!" shouted a poodle.

"How funny he looks!" cried a Dalmatian.

Boris was very embarrassed. He walked back to his place with his head drooped and his tails to the floor.

**10** Why did the Dalmatian think Boris looked funny?

_____

1 mark

**11** How does the text say Boris felt when the others laughed at him?

_____

1 mark

A moment later, he sneaked out of the room and into the entrance hall, where he saw a poster for a dog show. Boris read it aloud.

"Prizes for cutest face, shiniest coat, *most waggly tail*… I'll show them," he said with a grin.

---

**12** What did Boris do when he saw the poster? Tick **one** box.

He started howling. ☐   He walked out the door. ☐

He called to the others. ☐   He read it aloud. ☐

1 mark

**13** Which of these do you think will happen at the dog show? Tick **one** box.

Boris will be trained to be a better dog. ☐   Boris will not enter the show. ☐

Boris will win the most waggly tail prize. ☐   Boris will chase the other animals. ☐

1 mark

# Useful Words

legend

Nottinghamshire

national

species

experts

# The Home of Robin Hood

According to legend, Robin Hood was a man who stole things from rich people then gave these things to poor people.

Robin was good at fighting, and he had a group of followers called the 'Merry Men' who helped him.

## Practice Questions

**c** What happened to the things Robin Hood stole?

_____

**d** Who were the 'Merry Men'?  Tick **one** box.

- Robin Hood's victims ☐
- Robin Hood's brothers ☐
- Robin Hood's animals ☐
- Robin Hood's helpers ☐

People say that Robin Hood used to live in Sherwood Forest.

Sherwood Forest is an area of woodland in Nottinghamshire. It's a national nature reserve — this means that people are trying to protect the plants and animals found there.

Around 1500 species of beetle and roughly 200 different types of spider live in Sherwood Forest.

---

**14** What is a *nature reserve*? Tick **one** box.

a city near Sherwood Forest ☐

a place where plants and animals are protected ☐

a park in Nottinghamshire ☐

a forest where people live with animals ☐

1 mark

**15** Name **two** animals that live in Sherwood Forest.

1. _____

2. _____

1 mark

A famous tree called 'The Major Oak' can be found in Sherwood Forest, and this tree is believed to have been Robin Hood's hideout. People guess that The Major Oak is between 800 and 1000 years old.

*The Major Oak*

A fence surrounds the tree to help protect it from visitors. This fence is important because it stops visitors standing on the soil above the tree's roots.

Metal poles help support the tree's enormous branches, and tree experts regularly check to make sure that The Major Oak is healthy.

**16** Which word shows that people are uncertain about how old The Major Oak is? Tick **one** box.

- famous ☐
- guess ☐
- years ☐
- experts ☐

1 mark

**17** *Metal poles help support the tree's enormous branches*
What does the word *enormous* mean in this sentence?

_____

1 mark

**18** Who checks that The Major Oak is healthy?

_____

1 mark

According to the story of Robin Hood, if Robin wasn't at The Major Oak, then he was perhaps fighting his arch-enemy, the Sheriff of Nottingham.

The Sheriff of Nottingham was in charge of trying to capture criminals, like Robin Hood, to stop them from killing the King's deer and to keep Sherwood Forest safe.

**19** Why did Robin Hood dislike the Sheriff of Nottingham?

_____

_____

1 mark

**20** Look at the table below. Put a tick in each row to show whether each statement is true or false.
One has already been done for you.

| The information tells us that... | True | False |
|---|---|---|
| Robin Hood was always at the Major Oak. | | ✓ |
| Robin Hood was a criminal. | | |
| criminals tried to kill the King's deer. | | |

1 mark

**END OF TEST**

[Blank Page]

# Key Stage One English

## Set A
### Reading Paper 2
Reading Booklet

This booklet contains:
*Water in Britain*
*Going on Safari*

EHEP13

# Contents

Water in Britain..................................................pages 4-6

Going on Safari..................................................pages 7-10

# Water in Britain

Most people don't think about how much water they use. Each person in Britain uses about 150 litres of water a day — enough to fill around 455 drink cans!

## Why should people save water?

Most of the Earth's water is found in oceans or seas and is too salty to drink. This means that for every 100 litres of water on planet Earth, only 1 litre can be used for drinking and washing. So, as the amount of people in the world goes up, the amount of water for each person shrinks. The less water each person uses, the easier it is to prevent water shortages.

# How *you* can help

There are a number of ways people can save water at home.

### 1. Take showers instead of baths

The average shower lasts eight minutes and uses less water than having a bath. Special water-saving shower heads can also be fitted to make showers use even less water.

### 2. Don't run taps

Whether you're brushing your teeth or washing some vegetables, leaving a tap running wastes a lot of water. Partly fill up the sink if you plan to wash lots of items, and only turn the tap on in short bursts whilst brushing your teeth.

### 3. Use a dishwasher

Not only do they save time, but dishwashers use less water than washing plates and mugs by hand. Only put a dishwasher on when it's completely full though — otherwise you're wasting water, energy and money.

### 4. Place a plastic bottle in your toilet

Around a third of the water used by a household is used to flush toilets. By filling a plastic bottle with water and placing it in the top of your toilet, you can reduce the amount of water being used for each flush. The bottle takes up some of the space that would be filled with water if the bottle wasn't there.

### 5. Collect water in a water butt

Water butts are big plastic tubs which collect and store rainwater. This rainwater can then be used to water gardens or to fill up ponds.

### 6. Keep water in the fridge

Keeping a jug of water in the fridge stops you having to run the tap until it gets cold enough for a drink.

# GOING ON SAFARI

Helene loved animals. She had large posters of them stuck all over the walls of her bedroom, and her bookcase was full of books about them. Now on this very special holiday, her dream of going on safari and seeing some of her favourite animals was about to come true.

The sky was still dark as Helene got up and dressed. Helene and her mum, along with three other guests staying at the hotel, walked quietly through the hall and into the waiting truck. The tour guides had said that one of the best times to see animals was at dawn. They would be drinking from the main watering hole (a large pool) before they went off to find food.

The truck bounced and creaked as it travelled along the bumpy track. The windows had been taken out of the back of the truck so you could see the animals better. Helene was sure she would be glad about that later, but for now she pulled her jacket closer around her.

After what seemed like forever — but what was really about twenty minutes — the truck slowed down and the group could see the watering hole up ahead.  Helene gave her mum an excited grin.

As the sun rose, it showed a group of zebras drifting towards the water.  They looked around nervously before they dropped their heads and had a drink.  Helene grabbed the camera her uncle had bought her for her birthday and excitedly began taking pictures.

Just along from the stripy zebras, giraffes appeared.  Helene couldn't believe how large they were in real life.  Their necks stretched high into the sky, and their legs carried on for miles in the other direction.  Helene's mum laughed as the giraffes bent down to drink.  Their staggering height and long legs made it difficult for them to reach the water.  They had to spread their legs far apart to bend that far down.  They looked like they were going to fall over.

"We can try to get closer for a better look," said the guide. Helene was too excited to speak. Instead she just nodded eagerly. The truck circled the giant lake slowly, when suddenly it stopped.

Helene looked to the front of the truck and was amazed at what she saw. Ahead of them stood a huge elephant. It was looking straight at them. It flapped its grey, wrinkled ears and trumpeted loudly. A man sitting behind Helene let out a small cry. As quietly as he could, the guide began moving the truck backwards. The elephant kept staring, and Helene held her breath. The group kept moving further and further backwards until the elephant turned away. Helene finally let her breath go with a loud sigh.

The elephant called out towards the trees, and a line of elephants marched out from behind them. The first to appear was another large elephant. Just behind it was a baby elephant. Helene counted four more calves as they walked past with their mothers.

After the elephants had passed, the guide carried on towards the watering hole. The group got close to the zebras they had seen earlier. Helene took a few more pictures of them, but she was still thinking about the elephants. She could see that, not too far away, the younger elephants were playing in the water. The parents watched carefully.

As Helene and the others watched, the sun crept higher into the sky and the animals gradually began to leave the watering hole.

"I think it's time we headed back," said the guide. Helene didn't want to leave. This had been the best experience of her life. The truck turned and began its journey back to the hotel. Helene held her camera tightly. She would always have her pictures to remind her of this brilliant trip.

# Key Stage One English

## Set A
## Reading

### Paper 2: Answer Booklet

**Water in Britain**
**Going on Safari**

| First name | |
| --- | --- |
| Middle name | |
| Last name | |

**Total marks**

Exam Set EHEP13

*Water in Britain*

> **These questions are about *Water in Britain***

*(Page 4)*

**1** How many litres of water does a person in Britain use each day?

_____

1 mark

*(Page 4)*

**2** *...the easier it is to prevent water shortages.*

What does the word *prevent* mean in the sentence above?

Tick **one** box.

guess ☐

cause ☐

change ☐

stop ☐

1 mark

*(Page 5)*

**3** How long does an average shower last?

_____

1 mark

*Water in Britain*

(Page 5)

**4** How can a shower be changed to save even more water?

_____

_____

1 mark

(Pages 4-5)

**5** Look at the table below. Put a tick in each row to show whether each statement is **true** or **false**.

| The information tells us that... | True | False |
|---|---|---|
| people can safely drink salt water. | | |
| shorter showers help prevent water shortages. | | |

1 mark

(Page 5)

**6** Why is it a bad idea to run a dishwasher if it's half full?

Tick **one** box.

It wastes energy. ☐

It uses more water. ☐

It takes longer. ☐

It won't clean things properly. ☐

1 mark

*Water in Britain*

(Page 6)

**7** How much of the water used by a household is used to flush the toilet?

_____

1 mark

(Pages 5-6)

**8** What **two** things does the text suggest you could do to save water?

Tick **two** boxes.

Drink less water. ☐

Stop running the tap while brushing your teeth. ☐

Keep a jug of water in the fridge. ☐

Drink rain water. ☐

1 mark

*Going on Safari*

**These questions are about *Going on Safari***

**9** How can you tell that it was early in the morning when Helene got up?

(Page 7)

_____

1 mark

**10** When is one of the best times to see animals at the watering hole?

(Page 7)

_____

1 mark

**11** Why was Helene unhappy about the missing windows in the truck?

(Page 7)

_____

1 mark

*Going on Safari*

**12** *They looked around nervously before they dropped their heads...*
What does the word *nervously* mean in the sentence above?

Tick **one** box.

very quietly ☐

in a scared way ☐

for a long time ☐

without fear ☐

**13** Who bought Helene her camera?

_____

**14** Why did Helene's mum find the giraffes funny?

_____

_____

*Going on Safari*

(Pages 9-10)

**15** Why did the elephant flap its ears and trumpet at the group?

_____

_____

1 mark

(Page 9)

**16** a) How do you think Helene felt when the large elephant turned away from the truck?

_____

1 mark

b) How can you tell?

_____

_____

1 mark

(Page 10)

**17** What are baby elephants called?

_____

1 mark

*Going on Safari*

(Pages 7-10)

**18** Number these events in the order in which they happen in the story.

The first one has already been done.

| | |
|---|---|
| Helene saw giraffes. | ☐ |
| Helene and the group got into the truck. | 1 |
| Helene saw some elephants playing in the water. | ☐ |
| Helene saw zebras. | ☐ |
| Helene started taking pictures. | ☐ |

1 mark

(Page 11)

**19** *...and the animals gradually began to leave the watering hole.*

What does the word *gradually* mean in the sentence above?

Tick **one** box.

| | |
|---|---|
| all at once | ☐ |
| quickly | ☐ |
| slowly | ☐ |
| finally | ☐ |

1 mark

**END OF TEST**

# Key Stage One English

## Set A
## Grammar, Punctuation and Spelling

## Paper 2: Questions

| First name | |
|---|---|
| Middle name | |
| Last name | |

Paper 1, the spelling task, is a pull-out section in the middle of the booklet.

Total marks

## Practice Questions

**a** Draw a line to match each sentence with the most likely final punctuation mark. One has already been done for you.

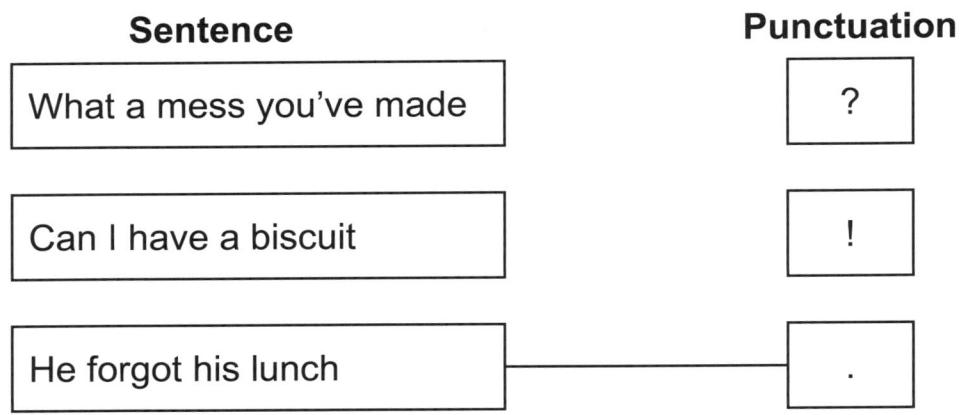

**b** Read the sentence below. **Circle** the **two nouns**.

*The hungry bear looked for tasty fish.*

**1** The sentence below is missing a **capital letter**.
Tick **one** box to show where the capital letter should go.

We are going to visit our friends in december.
☐ ☐ ☐ ☐

1 mark

**2** The sentence below is missing a punctuation mark.
Add the correct punctuation mark.

Why do you want to go there

1 mark

**3** Read the sentence below. What type of word is '**dog**'?

**The dog chased the cat down the road.**

Tick **one** box.

noun ☐

verb ☐

adjective ☐

adverb ☐

**4** The sentence below is missing a **comma**.
Tick **one** box to show where the comma should go.

**Elizabeth likes cheese chocolate and strawberries.**

**5** Read the sentence below. What type of word is '**quickly**'?

**Timothy quickly tidied his bedroom.**

Tick **one** box.

noun ☐

verb ☐

adjective ☐

adverb ☐

1 mark

**6** Add '**s**' or '**es**' to the words below to make them plural.

church____     frog____     bus____

1 mark

**7** Read the sentence below.
Put a tick in the box next to the word that **completes the sentence**.

**Ahmed enjoys fishing, _____ he hates swimming.**

          Tick **one** box.

because ☐

but ☐

when ☐

that ☐

**8** Read the sentence below. **Circle** the **two verbs**.

**Darius weeded the garden and cut the grass with his dad's lawn mower.**

# Key Stage One English

## Set A
## Grammar, Punctuation and Spelling

## Paper 1: Spelling

| First name | |
| Middle name | |
| Last name | |

**Total marks**

# Spelling Test

**Practice Question**

Jacob kicked a _____ along the floor.

---

1. I _____ my friends when I don't see them.

2. Socks keep your feet _____ .

3. James likes sailing on his _____ .

4. The wind _____ my paper onto the floor.

5. Charlotte is _____ than Loreen.

6. She climbed the _____ to go to bed.

7. Tom likes _____ jam on his toast.

8. The loud _____ hurt Eric's ears.

9. I put _____ in my porridge.

10. We might be _____ to help.

11. Maddy goes swimming every _____ .

12. I am wearing a _____ because it's cold.

13. Graham enjoyed _____ at the shop.

14. John made a _____ to the baker.

15. Urvi was the star _____ last week.

16. Kate has always been very _____ .

17. We had a _____ fight in the garden.

18. My brother _____ films about animals.

19. Kajal got _____ the more she heard.

20. My nan has a _____ in her garden.

**END OF TEST**

[Blank Page]

**9** Read the sentences below. Tick the sentence that is a **statement**.

Tick **one** box.

Where is my pencil case? ☐

The children played outside. ☐

Put the box on the floor. ☐

What a wonderful day we've had! ☐

1 mark

**10** Read the sentences below and circle the **full stops** that are wrong. One has already been done for you.

Marcus opened. his present. He was happy because. he got a new bike. His brother. George was jealous.

1 mark

**11** Read the sentence below. **Circle** the **three adjectives**.

There is a large, grumpy, stripy tiger on the loose.

1 mark

**12** Read the sentences below. Tick the sentence that is **correct**.

Tick **one** box.

I find a penny and gives it to Luke. ☐

I found a penny and give it to Luke. ☐

I find a penny and gave it to Luke. ☐

I found a penny and gave it to Luke. ☐

1 mark

**13** Read the sentence below.
Tick the **correct option** to complete the sentence.

**Yesterday, I was _____ my bike when it began to rain.**

Tick **one** box.

rode ☐

rides ☐

ride ☐

riding ☐

1 mark

**14** Read the sentences below.
Tick the sentence that is an **exclamation**.

Tick **one** box.

Where are you going on holiday? ☐

There's a strange car parked outside. ☐

Run away if you're chased by the dog! ☐

What an amazing adventure that was! ☐

1 mark

**15** Read the sentence below.

**Hadia was a very lucky girl.**

Add a prefix to the word <u>lucky</u> below so that the sentence means the opposite.

**Hadia was a very _____lucky girl.**

1 mark

**16** Make this sentence **past tense** by circling the right verbs.

**My brother | throws | threw | a ball and | knocks | knocked | over the lamp.**

1 mark

**17** Read the sentences below. Rewrite the underlined words in their short forms **using apostrophes**.
One has already been done for you.

| I'll |
↑
<u>I will</u> have to clean the house before Dad gets home.

[ ]   [ ]
 ↑      ↑
<u>They are</u> writing a story and <u>it is</u> about a dragon.

2 marks

**18** Annabelle would like a glass of water, so she tells her brother to get her one.

Write a **command** that Annabelle could give him in the speech bubble below. Use the correct punctuation.

2 marks

**END OF TEST**

[Blank Page]

# Key Stage One English

## Set B
## Reading

### Paper 1: Reading Prompt and Answer Booklet

| First name | |
|---|---|
| Middle name | |
| Last name | |

**Total marks**

Exam Set EHEP13

# Useful Words

tropical

rainforest

oxygen

species

Amazon

# Tropical Rainforests

Tropical rainforests are a type of rainforest. They are warm, wet forests where it rains a lot.

They are very important because the many trees create oxygen which we breathe.

## Practice Questions

a  Name a type of rainforest.

_____

b  Why are rainforests important?

_____

Rainforests only cover a small amount of the planet, but they are home to around half of the species of plants and animals that are found on Earth.

**1** How many of the Earth's plant and animal species are found in rainforests?

Tick **one** box.

around a third ☐

around a quarter ☐

around half ☐

around three-quarters ☐

1 mark

The largest rainforest is the Amazon rainforest. It is found in South America.

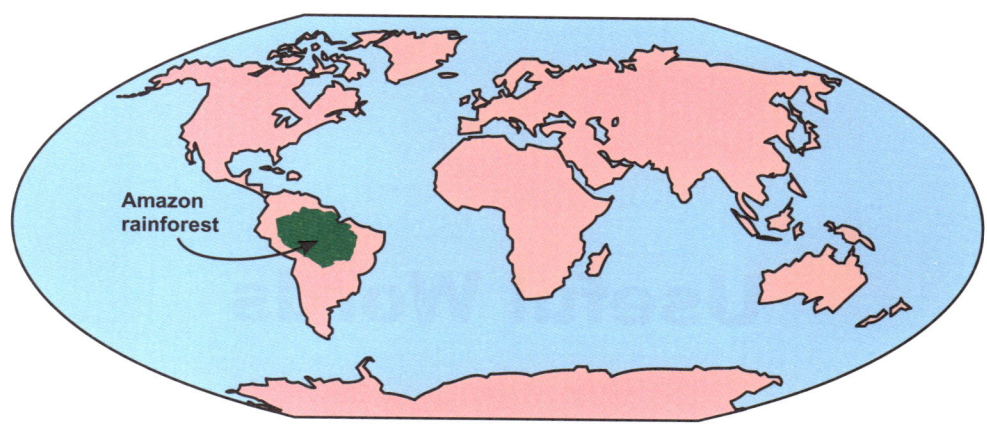

Around a fifth of the Amazon rainforest has been chopped down in the last 40 years.

Recently, countries in South America have been trying to reduce the number of trees they cut down.

---

**2** Where is the largest rainforest?

_____

1 mark

**3** How much of the Amazon rainforest has been chopped down in the last 40 years?

_____

1 mark

**4** *Recently, countries in South America have been trying to reduce the number of trees they cut down.*

What does the word *reduce* mean in this sentence?

_____

1 mark

# Useful Words

kayak

igloo

wriggling

squirming

# The Eagle and the Hunter

There was once an old man who lived by the sea. He never hunted for sport. He only hunted when he needed to.

If he caught an animal, he didn't waste any part of it. He used all the meat for food, and all the skin for making clothes or mending his kayak.

## Practice Questions

**c** Where did the old man live?

_____

**d** What did the old man do with animal skins?
Tick **one** box.

He threw them away. ☐    He made clothes and fixed his kayak with them. ☐

He ate them. ☐    He cooked them. ☐

One day, the old man was walking on the beach when he saw an eagle. The old man was hungry and food was hard to find.

He fired an arrow at the eagle and killed it. He took the eagle back to his tent.

**5** Why did the old man kill the eagle?

Tick **one** box.

The eagle was on the man's beach. ☐

He wanted to eat the eagle. ☐

The eagle had eaten all the food. ☐

The eagle wanted to fight. ☐

1 mark

The old man plucked the eagle's feathers and then cooked it over the fire.

The old man ate every scrap of meat on the eagle's body. He saved some bones to use as needles and fishing hooks. He burnt the rest in the fire.

---

**6** Draw lines to complete the sentences so they describe what the man did.

| He plucked | | the rest. |
| He saved | | the feathers. |
| He burnt | | some bones. |

1 mark

**7** Why did the old man eat every scrap of meat?

_____

1 mark

The next day, the old man went back to the sea. Two young eagles landed nearby. The old man aimed an arrow at the smaller eagle.

He was just about to shoot when, to his surprise, it spoke to him. "Our mother wants to meet you. Lie down on the ground so my brother and I can carry you to her igloo."

The old man lay down on the ground. The eagles grasped him firmly in their claws and carried him away.

**8** Which eagle was the old man going to shoot?

_____

1 mark

**9** Why was the old man surprised?

_____

1 mark

**10** Why did the eagle tell the old man to lie on the ground?

_____

1 mark

They flew high over the white mountains until they came to an igloo. The young eagles told the old man to go inside.

The mother eagle said, "I want to thank you. You killed my son, but you treated him well. You used all his meat for food and didn't even waste his bones. Tell me how I can reward you."

The old man said, "I am so very sorry for killing your son. I will not take any reward from you."

---

**11** **Find** and **copy** one word that shows the mountains were snowy.

_____

1 mark

**12** Why did the mother eagle want to thank the old man?

_____

1 mark

**13** Why did the old man say he would not take a reward?

_____

_____

1 mark

The mother eagle showed the old man the heaps of warm furs she had in her igloo and said he must take something.

The old man did not want to make the mother eagle angry so he said that he would take some white fox furs.

**14** **Find** and **copy** one word that tells you there were lots of furs.

_____

**15** Why did the old man take the white fox furs?

Tick **one** box.

He did not want to make the eagle angry. ☐

He was very cold. ☐

He was sorry for killing the eagle's son. ☐

He had always wanted white fox furs. ☐

The mother eagle took all her white fox furs down from the shelf. "You've chosen well. These furs have magical powers." she declared.

She put the furs in a bag and gave it to the old man, saying, "My sons will take you home now. They will take you very near to your tent, but you must walk the last part of the journey alone."

**16** Why were the fox furs special?

_____

1 mark

**17** What did the old man have to do on his own?
Tick **one** box.

leave the igloo ☐   kill another eagle ☐

walk to his tent ☐   sew the furs together ☐

1 mark

"If you feel thirsty and have to take a drink, keep your eyes closed. Do not look into the water — it will break the spell on the furs," the mother eagle warned.

The eagles flew the old man back over the mountains and left him a little way from his tent.

After the old man had walked for a few minutes he felt very thirsty.

---

**18** Number these events in the order in which they happen in the story.

The first one has already been done.

The eagle's mother gave the man some furs. ☐

The old man shot, cooked and ate an eagle. [1]

The old man was warned not to look into water. ☐

The old man met the eagle's family. ☐

1 mark

He came to a stream and bent down to drink. Too thirsty to remember the mother eagle's words, he looked straight into the cool, bright water.

Suddenly, the old man felt something wriggling and squirming in the bag hanging from his shoulder. A loud howl echoed around him.

**19** Why did the old man look into the stream?

Tick **one** box.

| He wanted to break the spell. ☐ | He forgot the eagle's words. ☐ |
| He thought the eagle was a liar. ☐ | He was angry with the eagle. ☐ |

1 mark

**20** What do you think happens next in the story?

_____

_____

1 mark

**END OF TEST**

[Blank Page]

# Contents

The Moving Picture Show..................................................pages 4-9

Owls......................................................................page 10

The Frosted Pane..........................................................page 11

# The Moving Picture Show

Today there is a cinema in nearly every town and city, and millions of people go to the cinema every week. Until 1896, there were no cinemas in Britain. People had never seen moving pictures.
This is a story about a boy called Paul who saw one of the first films ever made.

A long time ago, a boy called Paul lived with his mum, his dad and his grandpa. They lived in a small flat on the fourth floor of a tall, narrow house.

In the school holidays, Paul worked at a fruit and vegetable market. It was his job to deliver fruit and vegetables to cafes near the market.

One day, as Paul was wrapping a melon in newspaper, a large advertisement caught his eye.

> For one night only!
> The Lumiere brothers
> present their amazing new invention
> ## The Moving Picture Show
> at the
> Grand Cafe
> 28 December 1895, 6 o'clock sharp

Paul had heard people talking about moving pictures — at school, at home and in the market. Nobody had seen them yet, but everybody had heard stories about the Lumiere brothers and their magic cameras. He longed to be one of the first people in the world to see a moving picture, but the Grand Cafe was a very smart place, and Paul was always wearing dirty work clothes.

"Oh well," Paul sighed. He finished wrapping the melon, popped it in a basket and delivered it on his way home.

When Paul arrived home, supper was on the table. It was his favourite — onion soup. But Paul just stared into his bowl and stirred it round and round.

Paul's mum asked him what was wrong.
"It's not important," said Paul. "But I do want to go."
"Where do you want to go?"
"The moving picture show. It's at six o'clock tomorrow night at the Grand Cafe. How can a scruffy market boy like me go to the Grand Cafe?"
"I've got an idea," said Grandpa. "Don't you deliver fruit and vegetables to the Grand Cafe?"
"Yes…" said Paul.
"Tomorrow night, make your delivery to the Grand Cafe just before six. From the kitchen it will be easy to get into the cafe."
"Of course, Grandpa," Paul cried. "What a brilliant idea!"

The next day, just before six o'clock, Paul said goodbye to his boss and set off to the Grand Cafe with a neatly packed box of fruit and vegetables.

Paul squeezed through the crowds milling around in front of the cafe and went down a side alley to the kitchen door. The kitchen was empty so he left the fruit and vegetables on a table, then walked straight through the main doors into the cafe itself.

The cafe was packed. Everyone was talking in loud voices, and looking at a big white sheet hung over a stage at the far end of the room.
Nobody was looking at Paul, but he hid himself behind a big leafy plant just in case.
Two men in top hats climbed onto the stage.
"The Lumiere brothers," Paul gasped.

The room fell silent. One of the men took off his hat and announced, "We proudly present the world's first moving picture!" Everyone clapped and the lights went out.

A wide silvery beam of light shone through the darkness onto a sheet. Paul heard a faint whirring noise and a picture appeared. Paul could see a railway station. People were waiting for a train.

"Wow," Paul said to himself. "That woman's scarf is flapping in the breeze! The picture really is moving – it's just like being there!" In the distance, down the railway track, a little speck was getting larger and larger. It was a train, coming closer... and closer... and closer.

A woman in the front row screamed. Several people stood up and started pushing towards the back of the cafe. They were terrified. They thought the train was going to burst into the cafe.

Paul felt a bit nervous himself, but he couldn't stop staring at the screen. The train slowed down and stopped. People got on and off. As quickly as it had begun, the film was over. The words "The End" appeared on the screen, and the lights came back on. The people who had stood up because they were afraid sat down again slowly. They looked like they wanted to hide.

Paul sneaked back through the kitchen onto the street. All the way home he played the film over and over in his head. It was a picture he would never forget.

## The End

# Owls

Owls are nocturnal birds. This means that they hunt for food at night and sleep during the day. There are over 200 kinds of owl.

## Appearance

Different kinds of owl come in different sizes, and their feathers can also vary. Barn owls have snowy white and pale brown feathers. They are about 34 cm tall. Tawny owls are larger (about 40 cm tall) and have speckled brown feathers.

The tawny owl's speckles help the owl to blend into the background so that its prey doesn't notice that it's there.

A Barn Owl

A Tawny Owl

## Habitat

Barn owls like to hunt in open fields and grassland, so they are often found nesting on farms. Tawny owls prefer to hunt in woods and hedgerows.

Some types of owl are in danger of dying out, so wildlife groups have been set up to help protect them. These groups often put nesting boxes on trees. They choose trees in woodland or near open fields.

# The Frosted Pane

When I wakened, very early,

All my window-pane was pearly

With a sparkling little picture traced in lines of shining white;

Some magician with a gleaming

Frosty brush, while I was dreaming,

Must have come and by the starlight worked through all the quiet night.


He had painted frosty people,

And a frosty church and steeple,

And a frosty bridge and river tumbling over frosty rocks;

Frosty mountain peaks that glimmered,

And fine frosty ferns that shimmered,

And a frosty little pasture full of frosty little flocks.


It was all touched in so lightly

And it glittered, oh, so whitely,

That I gazed and gazed in wonder at the lovely painted pane;

Then the sun rose high and higher

With his wand of golden fire

Till, alas, my picture vanished and I looked for it in vain!


Evaleen Stein

# Key Stage One English

## Set B Reading

## Paper 2: Answer Booklet

**The Moving Picture Show**
**Owls**
**The Frosted Pane**

| First name | |
|---|---|
| Middle name | |
| Last name | |

**Total marks**

Exam Set EHEP13

*The Moving Picture Show*

**These questions are about *The Moving Picture Show***

(Page 4)

**1** Which three relatives did Paul live with?

_____

1 mark

(Page 4)

**2** What did Paul do with fruit and vegetables?

_____

_____

1 mark

(Page 5)

**3** When were the Lumiere brothers going to present their new invention?

_____

1 mark

*The Moving Picture Show*

(Page 5)

**4** Why did Paul think that he wouldn't be able to go to see The Moving Picture Show?

Tick **one** box.

He had to go to school. ☐

The Grand Cafe would be closed. ☐

He had to go to work. ☐

He had no smart clothes to wear. ☐

(Page 6)

**5** How can Paul's mum tell that Paul isn't happy?

_____

_____

(Page 6)

**6** **Find** and **copy** a word that tells you that Paul thinks his Grandpa's idea is great.

_____

*The Moving Picture Show*

(Page 7)

**7**  Number these events in the order in which they happen.
The first one has been done for you.

Paul enters the cafe itself. ☐

Paul leaves work and heads towards the Grand Cafe. `1`

Paul hides behind a plant. ☐

The Lumiere brothers come onto the stage. ☐

Paul goes into the cafe's kitchen. ☐

1 mark

(Page 8)

**8**  What **two** sounds did Paul hear in the cafe?

Tick **two** boxes.

the train's wheels ☐

the audience clapping ☐

a whirring noise ☐

a train's whistle ☐

the wind ☐

1 mark

*The Moving Picture Show*

**9** Why did the people who stood up look like they wanted to hide?

(Page 9)

_____

_____

1 mark

**10** a) Think about the story you have just read.
If another moving picture show came to Paul's town, what do you think Paul would do?

(Pages 4-9)

_____

_____

1 mark

b) How can you tell?

_____

_____

1 mark

*Owls*

**These questions are about *Owls***

(Page 10)

**11** What do nocturnal animals do during the day?

_____

What do they do at night?

_____

1 mark

(Page 10)

**12** *Tawny owls are larger (about 40 cm tall) and have speckled brown feathers.*

What does *speckled* mean in this sentence?  Tick **one** box.

covered in small spots ☐    covered in freckles ☐

covered in hairs ☐    covered in feathers ☐

1 mark

(Page 10)

**13** Draw a line to match each fact to the correct type of owl.

| hunts in woods and hedgerows | barn owl |

| hunts in open fields and grassland | tawny owl |

1 mark

*Owls*

**14** Look at the table below. Put a tick in each row to show whether each statement is true or false. (Page 10)

One has already been done for you.

| The information tells us that... | True | False |
|---|---|---|
| owls hunt for food at night. | ✓ | |
| barn owls have black feathers. | | |
| tawny owls blend into the background. | | |

1 mark

**15** Why might wildlife groups put nesting boxes near open fields? (Page 10)

_____

_____

1 mark

*The Frosted Pane*

> These questions are about *The Frosted Pane*

(Page 11)

**16** A picture made of ice is described in the poem. Where has it appeared?

_____

1 mark

(Page 11)

**17** In the poem, who has worked *all the quiet night*?

_____

1 mark

(Page 11)

**18** **Find** and **copy** one word that tells you there are animals in the picture.

_____

1 mark

(Page 11)

**19** What happened to the picture when the sun came? Tick **one** box.

It blew away. ☐    It melted away. ☐

It washed away. ☐    It became clearer. ☐

1 mark

**END OF TEST**

# Key Stage One English

## Set B
## Grammar, Punctuation and Spelling

### Paper 2: Questions

| First name | |
|---|---|
| Middle name | |
| Last name | |

Paper 1, the spelling task, is a pull-out section in the middle of the booklet.

**Total marks**

Exam Set EHEP13

## Practice Questions

**a** Read the sentence below. The arrow shows where a punctuation mark should be. Tick the punctuation mark that's missing.

*The pet shop had fish↑ hamsters and puppies.*

Tick **one** box.

comma ☐

full stop ☐

question mark ☐

apostrophe ☐

**b** Read the sentence below. Write a word in the gap to complete the sentence in the **past tense**.

*On Thursday, James _____ football after school.*

**1** The sentences below are missing a **full stop**.
Tick **one** box to show where the full stop should go.

Yesterday we went to the beach I built a sandcastle.

☐ ☐ ☐ ☐

1 mark

**2** Read the sentence below. Tick **one** word to correctly complete the sentence.

They said _____ it was the best cake in the world.

Tick **one** box.

if ☐

when ☐

because ☐

that ☐

1 mark

**3** The sentence below is missing a punctuation mark.
Add the correct punctuation mark.

**Would you like me to help you**

1 mark

**4** Read the sentence below and **circle** the **two nouns**.

**The glass vase was stored on the highest shelf.**

1 mark

**5** Read the sentence below. What type of word is '**neatly**'?

**Grant usually writes neatly at school.**

Tick **one** box.

verb ☐

adverb ☐

noun ☐

adjective ☐

1 mark

**6** The sentence below is missing **capital letters**.
Circle the **three** words that should have capital letters.

**my friend jane and i go to tennis lessons together.**

1 mark

**7** Read the sentence below and finish it by adding a **suffix** to the word **quiet**.

Sita closed the door  quiet_____  behind her.

1 mark

**8** Read the sentence below. **Circle** the **two verbs**.

She finished her picture and then tidied the paints.

1 mark

# Key Stage One English

## Set B
## Grammar, Punctuation and Spelling

## Paper 1: Spelling

| First name | |
| Middle name | |
| Last name | |

**Total marks**

Exam Set EHEP13

# Spelling Test

**Practice Question**

Phillip had to _____ out his old toys.

1. Elephants are _____ animals.

2. He wanted to _____ Jo for her help.

3. The fairy waved her magic _____ .

4. She was quick to _____ to my letter.

5. I can _____ a strange noise.

6. My dad is always _____ in the shower.

7. Karen took the _____ sticker off the present.

8. I have milk and _____ in my tea.

9. The tour guide knew lots of _____ information.

10. We asked Orisa if she was _____ to the park.

11. The fancy dress party had a pirate _____ .

12. Anton's house was in a deep _____ .

13. The _____ on the flower were bright pink.

14. Aaron dreamt of growing up to be an ice _____ .

15. Finish your pot before the clay _____ .

16. A unicycle only has one _____ .

17. I picked the best _____ at the time.

18. Ben got up at his _____ time of 7am.

19. He took a picture to _____ the monster was real.

20. Zahra _____ her auntie's birthday present.

**END OF TEST**

[Blank Page]

**9** Read the options below.
Put a tick by the option that is a correct **sentence**.

Tick **one** box.

The large, brown dog. ☐

Sally to the zoo last weekend. ☐

Harvey and Poppy, who are my cousins. ☐

He swam 5 km for charity. ☐

1 mark

**10** Read the sentence below. What type of word is '**almighty**'?

**The almighty tree blocked out the sun.**

Tick **one** box.

noun ☐

adverb ☐

adjective ☐

verb ☐

1 mark

**11** The sentence below is missing a punctuation mark.
Tick the correct punctuation mark.

**What a brilliant idea that is**

Tick **one** box.

exclamation mark ☐

full stop ☐

question mark ☐

apostrophe ☐

1 mark

**12** Read the sentences below. Tick the word to show what type of sentences they are.

> Go left at the post office.
> Walk towards the church.
> Cross the big red bridge.
> Turn right at the school.

Tick **one** box.

questions ☐

statements ☐

exclamations ☐

commands ☐

1 mark

**13** Read the sentence below. Tick **one** word to complete the sentence so that it is correct.

Louise _____ the flowers to Polly and smiled.

Tick **one** box.

give ☐

gave ☐

gives ☐

giving ☐

1 mark

**14** Look at the table below. Put a tick in each row to show whether the sentence is in the **present tense** or the **past tense**.

| Sentence | Present tense | Past tense |
|---|---|---|
| She is skipping in the park. | | |
| Azmin was singing. | | |
| I am cooking dinner. | | |

1 mark

**15** Use an **apostrophe** to write the words <u>was not</u> as one word.

That _____ **Luke's sister.**

1 mark

**16** The words in boxes are verbs in the **present tense**.
Fill in the gaps by writing these verbs in the **past tense**.
One has already been done for you.

| speak |
↓

**I** _____spoke_____ **English and German.**

| play |
↓

**Cameron** _____ **tennis with his uncle.**

| come |
↓

**The horses** _____ **over to see us.**

2 mark

**17** Tick the option below that is a **phrase** and **not** a **full sentence**.

Tick **one** box.

they ran home ☐

I arrived quickly ☐

the boy sang loudly ☐

the large blue house ☐

1 mark

**18** Phillip wants to know where Juliet is, so he asks his brother, Brian.

Write a **question** that Phillip could ask Brian in the speech bubble below. Use the correct punctuation.

2 marks

**END OF TEST**

[Blank Page]

# CGP

# Key Stage One
# English
## SATS Practice Papers

## Instructions with Answers & Mark Scheme

### Contents
Test Contents .................................................................................................. 3
Marking the Tests ............................................................................................ 3
Reading Test Answers ...................................................................................... 4
Grammar, Punctuation and Spelling Paper 1 Scripts/Answers ........................ 12
Grammar, Punctuation and Spelling Paper 2 Answers .................................... 16

Exam Set EHEP13

# Practice is the best way to prepare for the KS1 English SATs...

...and this brilliant pack from CGP is bursting with the most realistic SATs practice you'll find, all fully up to date for the latest tests!

It contains two full sets of Practice Papers, each including two reading papers and two grammar, punctuation and spelling papers — just like the real test pupils will take in Year 2.

We've also included answers and mark schemes in this booklet. That means it's easy to find out which areas are their strongest, and what they need to concentrate on ahead of the SATs.

---

Published by CGP

Editors: Chloe Anderson, Alex Fairer, Heather Gregson, Frances Rooney, James Summersgill, Rebecca Tate

Many thanks to Holly Poynton, Emma Crighton, Catherine Heygate and Amanda MacNaughton for the proofreading.
Also thanks to Laura Jakubowski for the copyright research.

Acknowledgements for Answer Booklet
National Curriculum references on pages 4, 6, 8, 10, 12, 13, 16 and 18 reproduced under the terms of the Open Government Licence. v3.0 http://www.nationalarchives.gov.uk/doc/open-government-licence/version/3/

Acknowledgements for Reading Set A, Paper 1:
With thanks to iStock for permission to use the image on page 13.

Acknowledgements for Reading Set A, Paper 2:
With thanks to iStock for permission to use the images on pages 1, 2, 3, 4, 5, 6, 7, 8, 9, 10, 11 and 12.

Acknowledgements for Reading Set B, Paper 1:
With thanks to iStock for permission to use the image on page 3.

Acknowledgements for Reading Set B, Paper 2:
Poem, The Frosted Pane, on page 11 by Evaleen Stein.
With thanks to iStock for permission to use the images on pages 1, 2, 3, 11 and 12.

Clipart from Corel®
Printed by Elanders Ltd, Newcastle upon Tyne.

Text, design, layout and original illustrations
© Coordination Group Publications Ltd. (CGP) 2017
All rights reserved.

**Photocopying more than 5% of a paper is not permitted, even if you have a CLA licence.
Extra copies are available from CGP with next day delivery • 0800 1712 712 • www.cgpbooks.co.uk**

KS1 English — Answers & Mark Scheme

# Test Contents

There are **two sets** of practice papers in this pack.
Each set has:

**Reading Paper 1**
About 30 minutes                                             **20 marks**
(combined booklet: reading, and question and answer booklet)

*Reading Paper 1 includes useful vocabulary and practice questions for you to discuss with pupils to get them started.*

**Reading Paper 2**
About 40 minutes                                             **20 marks**
(reading booklet, and question and answer booklet)

**Grammar, Punctuation and Spelling Paper 1 (Spelling)**
About 15 minutes                                             **20 marks**
(pull-out question and answer booklet)

*The spelling task needs to be read out to the child sitting the test. The spelling task scripts can be found on pages 14 and 15 of this booklet.*

**Grammar, Punctuation and Spelling Paper 2**
About 20 minutes                                             **20 marks**
(question and answer booklet)

*Again, there are practice questions in this paper for pupils to do first.*

The given **time limits** are rough **estimates** for the time needed to complete each paper. If you think a child needs more or less time, that's fine.

# Marking the Tests

The scores for these practice papers will give you a pretty good idea of whether a pupil is on track to achieve the **expected standard** in **Reading** and in **Grammar, Punctuation and Spelling**.

**Reading**

| | Marks available | |
|---|---|---|
| Paper 1: | 20 | There's a total of **40** marks available. |
| Paper 2: | 20 | The mark needed to achieve the **expected standard** varies from year to year, but if they get a total of **22** or more then they should be on track. |
| Total: | **40** | |

**Grammar, Punctuation and Spelling**

| | Marks available | |
|---|---|---|
| Paper 1: | 20 | Add up the marks in the two papers to give a score out of **40**. |
| Paper 2: | 20 | |
| Total: | **40** | Again, the **expected standard** will vary each year, but if they get a total score of **25** or more, they should be on track. |

# Set A: Reading Paper 1

## Content Domain Coverage

The table below shows the aspects of reading assessed in Set A reading paper 1.

| | 1a<br>Draw on knowledge of vocabulary to understand texts. | 1b<br>Identify and explain key aspects of fiction and non-fiction texts, such as characters, events, titles and information. | 1c<br>Identify and explain the sequence of events in texts. | 1d<br>Make inferences from the text. | 1e<br>Predict what might happen on the basis of what has been read so far. |
|---|---|---|---|---|---|
| Qu. | | | Section 1 — Boris the Dog | | |
| 1 | | 1 | | | |
| 2 | | 1 | | | |
| 3 | | 1 | | | |
| 4 | | 1 | | | |
| 5 | 1 | | | | |
| 6 | | | | 1 | |
| 7 | 1 | | | | |
| 8 | | | | 1 | |
| 9 | | 1 | | | |
| 10 | | 1 | | | |
| 11 | | 1 | | | |
| 12 | | 1 | | | |
| 13 | | | | | 1 |
| Qu. | | | Section 2 — The Home of Robin Hood | | |
| 14 | | 1 | | | |
| 15 | | 1 | | | |
| 16 | 1 | | | | |
| 17 | 1 | | | | |
| 18 | | 1 | | | |
| 19 | | | | 1 | |
| 20 | | | | 1 | |

## Set A: Reading Paper 1 — Answers

Section 1 — Boris the Dog

| Qu. | Requirement | Guidance | Marks (Domain) |
|---|---|---|---|
| a | typical | | — (1a) |
| b | Reference to sleeping / napping. | | — (1b) |
| 1 | Reference to his paws / feet. | | 1 (1b) |
| 2 | Reference to the day he went dog training. | | 1 (1b) |
| 3 | Reference to wagging his tails.<br>Reference to finding it difficult to walk.<br>Reference to being unable to keep his balance / wobbling like jelly. | Award 1 mark for reference to any of the acceptable answers. | 1 (1b) |

KS1 English — Answers & Mark Scheme

© CGP 2017

| Qu. | Requirement | Guidance | Marks (Domain) |
|---|---|---|---|
| 4 | Reference to the fact that his two tails were swinging in opposite directions.<br>**Do not accept** references to being excited. | | 1<br>(1b) |
| 5 | wobbled | | 1<br>(1a) |
| 6 | Boris was sitting on his tails. | | 1<br>(1d) |
| 7 | welcoming<br>cheerful<br>**Do not accept** sniff or woof. | Award 1 mark for both correct. | 1<br>(1a) |
| 8 | He went up to the trainer. | | 1<br>(1d) |
| 9 | Reference to gasps / sounds of surprise.<br>Reference to laughter. | Award 1 mark for both correct. | 1<br>(1b) |
| 10 | Reference to the fact that he has two tails. | | 1<br>(1b) |
| 11 | embarrassed | | 1<br>(1b) |
| 12 | He read it aloud. | | 1<br>(1b) |
| 13 | Boris will win the most waggly tail prize. | | 1<br>(1e) |

## Section 2 — The Home of Robin Hood

| Qu. | Requirement | Guidance | Marks (Domain) |
|---|---|---|---|
| c | Reference to the stolen things being given to poor people. | | —<br>(1b) |
| d | Robin Hood's helpers | | —<br>(1b) |
| 14 | a place where plants and animals are protected | | 1<br>(1b) |
| 15 | beetles<br>spiders | Award 1 mark for both correct. | 1<br>(1b) |
| 16 | guess | | 1<br>(1a) |
| 17 | Recognition that it refers to the large size of the branches. | | 1<br>(1a) |
| 18 | tree experts | | 1<br>(1b) |
| 19 | Reference to the idea that the Sheriff wanted to capture him.<br>Reference to the Sheriff trying to stop Robin from killing the King's deer.<br>**Do not accept** reference to the Sheriff being Robin's arch-enemy. | Award 1 mark for reference to either of the acceptable answers. | 1<br>(1d) |
| 20 | <table><tr><th>The information tells us that...</th><th>True</th><th>False</th></tr><tr><td>Robin Hood was always at the Major Oak.</td><td></td><td>✓</td></tr><tr><td>Robin Hood was a criminal.</td><td>✓</td><td></td></tr><tr><td>criminals tried to kill the King's deer.</td><td>✓</td><td></td></tr></table> | Award 1 mark for both correct. | 1<br>(1d) |

KS1 English — Answers & Mark Scheme

# Set A: Reading Paper 2

## Content Domain Coverage

The table below shows the aspects of reading assessed in Set A reading paper 2.

| Qu. | 1a<br>*Draw on knowledge of vocabulary to understand texts.* | 1b<br>*Identify and explain key aspects of fiction and non-fiction texts, such as characters, events, titles and information.* | 1c<br>*Identify and explain the sequence of events in texts.* | 1d<br>*Make inferences from the text.* | 1e<br>*Predict what might happen on the basis of what has been read so far.* |
|---|---|---|---|---|---|
| | | | Section 1 — Water in Britain | | |
| 1 | | 1 | | | |
| 2 | 1 | | | | |
| 3 | | 1 | | | |
| 4 | | 1 | | | |
| 5 | | | | 1 | |
| 6 | | 1 | | | |
| 7 | | 1 | | | |
| 8 | | 1 | | | |
| Qu. | | | Section 2 — Going on Safari | | |
| 9 | | | | 1 | |
| 10 | | 1 | | | |
| 11 | | | | 1 | |
| 12 | 1 | | | | |
| 13 | | 1 | | | |
| 14 | | 1 | | | |
| 15 | | | | 1 | |
| 16a | | | | 1 | |
| 16b | | | | 1 | |
| 17 | | 1 | | | |
| 18 | | | 1 | | |
| 19 | 1 | | | | |

## Set A: Reading Paper 2 — Answers

Section 1 — Water in Britain

| Qu. | Requirement | Guidance | Marks (Domain) |
|---|---|---|---|
| 1 | *150* | | 1 (1b) |
| 2 | *stop* | | 1 (1a) |
| 3 | *8 minutes* | | 1 (1b) |
| 4 | *Reference to the fact that a shower can be fitted with a special water-saving shower head.* | | 1 (1b) |

| Qu. | Requirement | | | Guidance | Marks (Domain) |
|---|---|---|---|---|---|
| 5 | The information tells us that... | True | False | Award 1 mark for both correct. | 1 (1d) |
| | people can safely drink salt water. | | ✓ | | |
| | shorter showers help prevent water shortages | ✓ | | | |
| 6 | It wastes energy. | | | | 1 (1b) |
| 7 | around a third | | | | 1 (1b) |
| 8 | Stop running the tap while brushing your teeth. Keep a jug of water in the fridge. | | | Award 1 mark for both correct. | 1 (1b) |

## Section 2 — Going on Safari

| Qu. | Requirement | Guidance | Marks (Domain) |
|---|---|---|---|
| 9 | Reference to the sky being dark. | | 1 (1d) |
| 10 | dawn | | 1 (1b) |
| 11 | Reference to her being cold / the missing windows letting the cold in. | | 1 (1d) |
| 12 | in a scared way | | 1 (1a) |
| 13 | her uncle | | 1 (1b) |
| 14 | Reference to the fact that it was difficult for them to reach the water / they had their legs spread far apart / they looked like they were going to fall over. **Do not accept** reference to the giraffes looking funny without an explanation. | Award 1 mark for reference to any of the acceptable answers. | 1 (1b) |
| 15 | Reference to the elephant trying to scare them away from the baby elephants / feeling under threat / warning the other elephants that they were there. | Award 1 mark for reference to any of the acceptable answers. | 1 (1d) |
| 16a | Reference to feeling relieved / pleased. | | 1 (1d) |
| 16b | She stopped holding her breath | | 1 (1d) |
| 17 | calves | | 1 (1b) |
| 18 | Helene saw giraffes. — 4<br>Helene and the group got into the truck. — 1<br>Helene saw some elephants playing in the water. — 5<br>Helene saw zebras. — 2<br>Helene started taking pictures. — 3 | Award 1 mark for all 4 correct. | 1 (1c) |
| 19 | slowly | | 1 (1a) |

# Set B: Reading Paper 1

## Content Domain Coverage

The table below shows the aspects of reading assessed in Set B reading paper 1.

| | 1a<br>Draw on knowledge of vocabulary to understand texts. | 1b<br>Identify and explain key aspects of fiction and non-fiction texts, such as characters, events, titles and information. | 1c<br>Identify and explain the sequence of events in texts. | 1d<br>Make inferences from the text. | 1e<br>Predict what might happen on the basis of what has been read so far. |
|---|---|---|---|---|---|
| Qu. | | | Section 1 — Tropical Rainforests | | |
| 1 | | 1 | | | |
| 2 | | 1 | | | |
| 3 | | 1 | | | |
| 4 | 1 | | | | |
| Qu. | | | Section 2 — The Eagle and the Hunter | | |
| 5 | | | | 1 | |
| 6 | | 1 | | | |
| 7 | | | | 1 | |
| 8 | | 1 | | | |
| 9 | | 1 | | | |
| 10 | | 1 | | | |
| 11 | 1 | | | | |
| 12 | | 1 | | | |
| 13 | | | | 1 | |
| 14 | 1 | | | | |
| 15 | | 1 | | | |
| 16 | | 1 | | | |
| 17 | | 1 | | | |
| 18 | | | 1 | | |
| 19 | | 1 | | | |
| 20 | | | | | 1 |

## Set B: Reading Paper 1 — Answers

Section 1 — Tropical Rainforests

| Qu. | Requirement | Guidance | Marks (Domain) |
|---|---|---|---|
| a | tropical | | — (1b) |
| b | They create oxygen / help us breathe | | — (1b) |
| 1 | around half | | 1 (1b) |
| 2 | South America<br>**Do not accept** in the Amazon | | 1 (1b) |
| 3 | around a fifth | | 1 (1b) |
| 4 | Recognition that it refers to decreasing the numbers of trees cut down. | | 1 (1a) |

KS1 English — Answers & Mark Scheme

© CGP 2017

# Section 2 — The Eagle and the Hunter

| Qu. | Requirement | Guidance | Marks (Domain) |
|---|---|---|---|
| c | by the sea | | — (1b) |
| d | He made clothes and fixed his kayak with them. | | — (1b) |
| 5 | He wanted to eat the eagle. | | 1 (1d) |
| 6 | He plucked — the feathers.<br>He saved — some bones.<br>He burnt — the rest. | Award 1 mark for all 3 correct. | 1 (1b) |
| 7 | Reference to the man feeling hungry.<br>Reference to there not being much food around. | Award 1 mark for reference to either of the acceptable answers. | 1 (1d) |
| 8 | the smaller eagle | | 1 (1b) |
| 9 | Reference to the eagle speaking / being able to speak.<br>**Do not accept** reference to the eagle carrying him. | | 1 (1b) |
| 10 | So they could carry him. | | 1 (1b) |
| 11 | white | | 1 (1a) |
| 12 | Reference to using every bit of his body / not wasting any part of him.<br>**Do not accept** reference to the mother being grateful without an explanation. | | 1 (1b) |
| 13 | Reference to feeling bad about killing the eagle's son.<br>Reference to feeling that he didn't deserve a reward. | Award 1 mark for reference to either of the acceptable answers. | 1 (1d) |
| 14 | heaps | | 1 (1a) |
| 15 | He did not want to make the eagle angry. | | 1 (1b) |
| 16 | They had magical powers. | | 1 (1b) |
| 17 | walk to his tent | | 1 (1b) |
| 18 | The eagle's mother gave the man some furs. — 3<br>The old man shot, cooked and ate an eagle. — 1<br>The old man was warned not to look into water. — 4<br>The old man met the eagle's family. — 2 | 1 mark for all 3 correct. | 1 (1c) |
| 19 | He forgot the eagle's words. | | 1 (1b) |
| 20 | Reference to the furs coming alive / foxes jumping out of the man's bag. | | 1 (1e) |

# Set B: Reading Paper 2

## Content Domain Coverage

The table below shows the aspects of reading assessed in Set B reading paper 2.

| | 1a<br>Draw on knowledge of vocabulary to understand texts. | 1b<br>Identify and explain key aspects of fiction and non-fiction texts, such as characters, events, titles and information. | 1c<br>Identify and explain the sequence of events in texts. | 1d<br>Make inferences from the text. | 1e<br>Predict what might happen on the basis of what has been read so far. |
|---|---|---|---|---|---|
| Qu. | | Section 1 — The Moving Picture Show | | | |
| 1 | | 1 | | | |
| 2 | | 1 | | | |
| 3 | | 1 | | | |
| 4 | | 1 | | | |
| 5 | | | | 1 | |
| 6 | 1 | | | | |
| 7 | | | 1 | | |
| 8 | | 1 | | | |
| 9 | | | | 1 | |
| 10a | | | | | 1 |
| 10b | | | | | 1 |
| Qu. | | Section 2 — Owls | | | |
| 11 | | 1 | | | |
| 12 | 1 | | | | |
| 13 | | 1 | | | |
| 14 | | 1 | | | |
| 15 | | | | 1 | |
| Qu. | | Section 3 — The Frosted Pane | | | |
| 16 | | 1 | | | |
| 17 | | 1 | | | |
| 18 | 1 | | | | |
| 19 | | | | 1 | |

## Set B: Reading Paper 2 — Answers

Section 1 — The Moving Picture Show

| Qu. | Requirement | Guidance | Marks (Domain) |
|---|---|---|---|
| 1 | his mum, his dad and his grandpa | | 1 (1b) |
| 2 | He delivers them to cafes near the market.<br>**Do not accept** reference to simply working at a vegetable market. | | 1 (1b) |
| 3 | on 28 December 1895 at 6 o'clock | | 1 (1b) |
| 4 | He had no smart clothes to wear. | | 1 (1b) |
| 5 | Reference to him not eating his soup. | | 1 (1d) |
| 6 | *cried* or *brilliant* | | 1 (1a) |

| Qu. | Requirement | Guidance | Marks (Domain) |
|---|---|---|---|
| 7 | Paul enters the cafe itself. — 3<br>Paul leaves work and heads towards the Grand Cafe. — 1<br>Paul hides behind a plant. — 4<br>The Lumiere brothers come onto the stage. — 5<br>Paul goes into the cafe's kitchen. — 2 | Award 1 mark for all 4 correct. | 1<br>(1c) |
| 8 | the audience clapping<br>a whirring noise | Award 1 mark for both correct. | 1<br>(1b) |
| 9 | Reference to feeling silly because they were afraid of a picture.<br>Reference to feeling embarrassed.<br>**Do not accept** reference to wanting to hide because they're terrified. | Award 1 mark for reference to either of the acceptable answers. | 1<br>(1d) |
| 10a | Reference to him trying to see that moving picture as well. | | 1<br>(1e) |
| 10b | Reference to him enjoying watching the one about the train. | | 1<br>(1e) |

## Section 2 — Owls

| Qu. | Requirement | Guidance | Marks (Domain) |
|---|---|---|---|
| 11 | They sleep during the day.<br>They hunt for food at night. | Award 1 mark for both correct. | 1<br>(1b) |
| 12 | covered in small spots | | 1<br>(1a) |
| 13 | hunts in woods and hedgerows — tawny owl<br>hunts in open fields and grassland — barn owl | | 1<br>(1b) |
| 14 | <table><tr><th>The information tells us that...</th><th>True</th><th>False</th></tr><tr><td>owls hunt for food at night.</td><td>✓</td><td></td></tr><tr><td>barn owls have black feathers.</td><td></td><td>✓</td></tr><tr><td>tawny owls blend into the background.</td><td>✓</td><td></td></tr></table> | Award 1 mark for both correct. | 1<br>(1b) |
| 15 | Reference to the fact that this is where some owls, such as barn owls, like to hunt.<br>**Do not accept** reference to protecting the owls. | | 1<br>(1d) |

## Section 3 — The Frosted Pane

| Qu. | Requirement | Guidance | Marks (Domain) |
|---|---|---|---|
| 16 | on a window | | 1<br>(1b) |
| 17 | some magician | | 1<br>(1b) |
| 18 | flocks | | 1<br>(1a) |
| 19 | It melted away. | | 1<br>(1d) |

KS1 English — Answers & Mark Scheme

# Grammar, Punctuation and Spelling Paper 1

## Content Domain Coverage
## Set A: Spelling

The table below shows the aspects of spelling assessed in Set A paper 1.

| Qu. | Spelling | Content domain reference | Mark |
|---|---|---|---|
| 1 | miss | S1 — the sounds 'f', 'l', 's', 'z' and 'k' spelt *ff*, *ll*, *ss*, *zz* and *ck* | 1 |
| 2 | warm | S32 — the 'or' sound spelt *ar* after *w* | 1 |
| 3 | boat | S8 — vowel digraphs and trigraphs | 1 |
| 4 | blew | S36 — homophones and near-homophones | 1 |
| 5 | taller | S7 — adding *-er* and *-est* to adjectives where no change is needed in the root word | 1 |
| 6 | stairs | S8 — vowel digraphs and trigraphs | 1 |
| 7 | cherry | S9 — words ending in *-y* | 1 |
| 8 | sound | S8 — vowel digraphs and trigraphs | 1 |
| 9 | honey | S28 — the 'u' sound spelt *o* | 1 |
| 10 | able | S18 — the 'l' or 'ul' sound spelt *-le* at the end of words | 1 |
| 11 | Tuesday | S13 — the days of the week | 1 |
| 12 | jacket | S1 — the sounds 'f', 'l', 's', 'z' and 'k' spelt *ff*, *ll*, *ss*, *zz* and *ck* | 1 |
| 13 | working | S31 — the 'er' sound spelt 'or' after *w* | 1 |
| 14 | payment | S34 — the suffixes *-ment*, *-ness*, *-ful*, *-less* and *-ly* | 1 |
| 15 | pupil | S21 — words ending in *-il* | 1 |
| 16 | active | S4 — the 'v' sound at the end of words | 1 |
| 17 | snowball | S12 — compound words | 1 |
| 18 | watches | S5 — adding *-s* and *-es* to words (plural of nouns and the third-person singular of verbs) | 1 |
| 19 | angrier | S24 — adding *-ed*, *-ing*, *-er* and *-est* to a root word ending in *-y* with a consonant before it | 1 |
| 20 | gnome | S16 — the 'n' sound spelt *kn-* and (less often) *gn-* at the beginning of words | 1 |

## Set B: Spelling

The table below shows the aspects of spelling assessed in Set B paper 1.

| Qu. | Spelling | Content domain reference | Mark |
|---|---|---|---|
| 1 | huge | S14 — the 'j' sound spelt as *-ge* and *-dge* at the end of words and sometimes spelt as *g* elsewhere in words before *e*, *i* and *y* | 1 |
| 2 | thank | S2 — the 'n' sound spelt *n* before *k* | 1 |
| 3 | wand | S30 — the 'o' sound spelt *a* after *w* and *q* | 1 |
| 4 | reply | S22 — the 'aye' sound spelt *-y* at the end of words | 1 |
| 5 | hear | S36 — homophones and near-homophones | 1 |
| 6 | singing | S6 — adding the endings *-ing*, *-ed* and *-er* to verbs where no change is needed in the root word | 1 |
| 7 | price | S15 — the 's' sound spelt *c* before *e*, *i* and *y* | 1 |
| 8 | sugar | S37 — common exception words | 1 |
| 9 | useful | S34 — the suffixes *-ment*, *-ness*, *-ful*, *-less* and *-ly* | 1 |
| 10 | coming | S25 — adding the endings *-ing*, *-ed*, *-er*, *-est* and *y* to words ending in *-e* with a consonant before it | 1 |
| 11 | theme | S8 — vowel digraphs and trigraphs | 1 |
| 12 | valley | S29 — the 'ee' sound spelt *-ey* | 1 |
| 13 | petals | S20 — the 'l' or 'ul' sound spelt *-al* at the end of words | 1 |
| 14 | skater | S11 — using 'k' for the *k* sound | 1 |
| 15 | dries | S23 — adding *-es* to nouns and verbs ending in *-y* | 1 |
| 16 | wheel | S10 — new consonant spellings *ph* and *wh* | 1 |
| 17 | option | S35 — words ending in *-tion* | 1 |
| 18 | usual | S33 — the 'zh' sound spelt *s* | 1 |
| 19 | prove | S37 — common exception words | 1 |
| 20 | wrapped | S17 — the 'r' sound spelt *wr* at the beginning of words | 1 |

# Guidance for Marking the Spelling Task

Here's some guidance for marking the paper 1 spelling tests:

- If the pupil makes more than one attempt, it needs to be clear which answer they wish to be marked. If the pupil makes two or more attempts and it isn't clear which is to be considered, the mark should not be awarded. Crossed-out answers that have not been replaced by another attempt should not be awarded a mark.
- Pupils can answer in lower or upper case, or a mixture of the two. However, days of the week must be written in lower-case letters with an initial capital letter.
- If the pupil has answered with the correct sequence of letters but has incorrectly inserted an apostrophe or a hyphen, the mark should not be awarded.
- If the pupil has answered with the correct sequence of letters but these have been separated into clearly divided components, with or without a hyphen, the mark should not be awarded.
- If a reversed letter has been used, it must be unambiguous for the mark to be awarded. You should refer to the pupil's handwriting in the rest of the test to decide whether or not the letter is ambiguous.

# Instructions for the Spelling Task

Each test should take about 15 minutes. This isn't a strict limit, so you can allow more time if needed.

Read out the following instructions, and answer any questions the children may have.

> - *Listen to the instructions I'm about to give you.*
> - *I'm going to read out a practice sentence. This sentence is printed at the top of your answer booklet, and it has a word missing. Listen to the missing word and write it in. Make sure you spell it correctly.*
> - *I will read the word, then read the word within a sentence, then I'll say the word a third time.*
> - *We will then stop and discuss as a class the word that you have written.*
> - *I will then read twenty more sentences to you. Each sentence is printed in your answer booklet and has a word missing. Listen to the missing word and write it in. Make sure you spell it correctly.*
> - *Have you got any questions?*

Now read the spellings to the children:

> - Say the spelling number (or *"Practice spelling"*)
> - Say *"The word is..."*
> - Read out the word in its sentence.
> - Say *"The word is..."*
> - Pause for at least 12 seconds between each of the spellings.
> - You may repeat the word again if needed.

At the end of the test, read out all 20 sentences again, and give the children time to change their answers if they want to.

When the test is over, say "This is the end of the test."

# Set A: Spelling — Script

> **Practice spelling** — the word is **stone**. *Jacob kicked a **stone** along the floor.* The word is **stone**.

**Spelling one** — the word is **miss**. *I **miss** my friends when I don't see them.* The word is **miss**.

**Spelling two** — the word is **warm**. *Socks keep your feet **warm**.* The word is **warm**.

**Spelling three** — the word is **boat**. *James likes sailing on his **boat**.* The word is **boat**.

**Spelling four** — the word is **blew**. *The wind **blew** my paper onto the floor.* The word is **blew**.

**Spelling five** — the word is **taller**. *Charlotte is **taller** than Loreen.* The word is **taller**.

**Spelling six** — the word is **stairs**. *She climbed the **stairs** to go to bed.* The word is **stairs**.

**Spelling seven** — the word is **cherry**. *Tom likes **cherry** jam on his toast.* The word is **cherry**.

**Spelling eight** — the word is **sound**. *The loud **sound** hurt Eric's ears.* The word is **sound**.

**Spelling nine** — the word is **honey**. *I put **honey** in my porridge.* The word is **honey**.

**Spelling ten** — the word is **able**. *We might be **able** to help.* The word is **able**.

**Spelling eleven** — the word is **Tuesday**. *Maddy goes swimming every **Tuesday**.* The word is **Tuesday**.

**Spelling twelve** — the word is **jacket**. *I am wearing a **jacket** because it's cold.* The word is **jacket**.

**Spelling thirteen** — the word is **working**. *Graham enjoyed **working** at the shop.* The word is **working**.

**Spelling fourteen** — the word is **payment**. *John made a **payment** to the baker.* The word is **payment**.

**Spelling fifteen** — the word is **pupil**. *Urvi was the star **pupil** last week.* The word is **pupil**.

**Spelling sixteen** — the word is **active**. *Kate has always been very **active**.* The word is **active**.

**Spelling seventeen** — the word is **snowball**. *We had a **snowball** fight in the garden.* The word is **snowball**.

**Spelling eighteen** — the word is **watches**. *My brother **watches** films about animals.* The word is **watches**.

**Spelling nineteen** — the word is **angrier**. *Kajal got **angrier** the more she heard.* The word is **angrier**.

**Spelling twenty** — the word is **gnome**. *My nan has a **gnome** in her garden.* The word is **gnome**.

# Set B: Spelling — Script

> **Practice spelling** — the word is **clear**. *Phillip had to **clear** out his old toys.* The word is **clear**.

**Spelling one** — the word is **huge**. *Elephants are **huge** animals.* The word is **huge**.

**Spelling two** — the word is **thank**. *He wanted to **thank** Jo for her help.* The word is **thank**.

**Spelling three** — the word is **wand**. *The fairy waved her magic **wand**.* The word is **wand**.

**Spelling four** — the word is **reply**. *She was quick to **reply** to my letter.* The word is **reply**.

**Spelling five** — the word is **hear**. *I can **hear** a strange noise.* The word is **hear**.

**Spelling six** — the word is **singing**. *My dad is always **singing** in the shower.* The word is **singing**.

**Spelling seven** — the word is **price**. *Karen took the **price** sticker off the present.* The word is **price**.

**Spelling eight** — the word is **sugar**. *I have milk and **sugar** in my tea.* The word is **sugar**.

**Spelling nine** — the word is **useful**. *The tour guide knew lots of **useful** information.* The word is **useful**.

**Spelling ten** — the word is **coming**. *We asked Orisa if she was **coming** to the park.* The word is **coming**.

**Spelling eleven** — the word is **theme**. *The fancy dress party had a pirate **theme**.* The word is **theme**.

**Spelling twelve** — the word is **valley**. *Anton's house was in a deep **valley**.* The word is **valley**.

**Spelling thirteen** — the word is **petals**. *The **petals** on the flower were bright pink.* The word is **petals**.

**Spelling fourteen** — the word is **skater**. *Aaron dreamt of growing up to be an ice **skater**.* The word is **skater**.

**Spelling fifteen** — the word is **dries**. *Finish your pot before the clay **dries**.* The word is **dries**.

**Spelling sixteen** — the word is **wheel**. *A unicycle only has one **wheel**.* The word is **wheel**.

**Spelling seventeen** — the word is **option**. *I picked the best **option** at the time.* The word is **option**.

**Spelling eighteen** — the word is **usual**. *Ben got up at his **usual** time of 7am.* The word is **usual**.

**Spelling nineteen** — the word is **prove**. *He took a picture to **prove** the monster was real.* The word is **prove**.

**Spelling twenty** — the word is **wrapped**. *Zahra **wrapped** her auntie's birthday present.* The word is **wrapped**.

# Set A: Grammar, Punctuation and Spelling Paper 2

## Content Domain Coverage

The table below shows the aspects of grammar, punctuation and spelling assessed in Set A paper 2.

| Qu. | Content domain reference | Mark |
|---|---|---|
| 1 | G5.1: Capital letters | 1 |
| 2 | G5.3: Question marks | 1 |
| 3 | G1.1: Nouns | 1 |
| 4 | G5.5: Commas in lists | 1 |
| 5 | G1.6: Adverbs | 1 |
| 6 | G6.3: Suffixes | 1 |
| 7 | G3.3: Co-ordinating conjunctions | 1 |
| 8 | G1.2: Verbs | 1 |
| 9 | G2.1: Statements | 1 |
| 10 | G5.2: Full stops | 1 |
| 11 | G1.3: Adjectives | 1 |
| 12 | G4.2: Tense consistency | 1 |
| 13 | G4.1d: Present and past progressive | 1 |
| 14 | G2.4: Exclamations | 1 |
| 15 | G6.2: Prefixes | 1 |
| 16 | G4.1a: Simple past and simple present | 1 |
| 17 | G5.8: Apostrophes | 2 |
| 18 | G2.3: Commands | 2 |

## Set A: Grammar, Punctuation and Spelling Paper 2 — Answers

| Qu. | Requirement | Guidance | Marks (Domain) |
|---|---|---|---|
| a | What a mess you've made — ! <br> Can I have a biscuit — ? | | — <br> (G5.4 <br> G5.3) |
| b | *bear* and *fish* | | — <br> (G1.1) |
| 1 | We are going to visit our friends in december. <br> ↑ <br> ✓ | | 1 <br> (G5.1) |
| 2 | ? | Award 1 mark for a question mark at the end of the sentence. | 1 <br> (G5.3) |
| 3 | noun | | 1 <br> (G1.1) |
| 4 | Elizabeth likes cheese chocolate and strawberries. <br> ↑ <br> ✓ | | 1 <br> (G5.5) |
| 5 | adverb | | 1 <br> (G1.6) |
| 6 | churches, frogs, buses | Award 1 mark for all 3 correct. | 1 <br> (G6.3) |
| 7 | but | | 1 <br> (G3.3) |

| Qu. | Requirement | Guidance | Marks (Domain) |
|---|---|---|---|
| 8 | *weeded* and *cut* | Award 1 mark for both correct. | 1 (G1.2) |
| 9 | *The children played outside.* | | 1 (G2.1) |
| 10 | *Marcus opened◯ his present. He was happy because◯ he got a new bike. His brother◯ George was jealous.* | Award 1 mark for both correct. | 1 (G5.2) |
| 11 | *large*, *grumpy* and *stripy* | Award 1 mark for all 3 correct. | 1 (G1.3) |
| 12 | *I found a penny and gave it to Luke.* | | 1 (G4.2) |
| 13 | *riding* | | 1 (G4.1d) |
| 14 | *What an amazing adventure that was!* | | 1 (G2.4) |
| 15 | *un* | The prefix must be spelt correctly. | 1 (G6.2) |
| 16 | *threw* and *knocked* | Award 1 mark for both correct. | 1 (G4.1a) |
| 17 | *They're, it's* | Award 1 mark for each correct answer. Answers must be spelt correctly. | 2 (G5.8) |
| 18 | *Answers may vary, for example:*<br>• *Get me a glass of water!*<br>• *Bring me a glass of water.*<br>**Do not accept** *answers in the form of a question or sentences that are grammatically incorrect or written in non-standard English.* | Award 2 marks for an appropriate command that is grammatically correct, with correct use of an initial capital letter and full stop or exclamation mark.<br>Award 1 mark for an appropriate command that is grammatically correct, with incorrect use of initial capital letter or full stop / exclamation mark.<br>No marks should be deducted for incorrect spelling. | 2 (G2.3) |

KS1 English — Answers & Mark Scheme

# Set B: Grammar, Punctuation and Spelling Paper 2

## Content Domain Coverage

The table below shows the aspects of grammar, punctuation and spelling assessed in Set B paper 2.

| Qu. | Content domain reference | Mark |
|---|---|---|
| 1 | G5.2: Full stops | 1 |
| 2 | G3.4: Subordinating conjunctions | 1 |
| 3 | G5.3: Question marks | 1 |
| 4 | G1.1: Nouns | 1 |
| 5 | G1.6: Adverbs | 1 |
| 6 | G5.1: Capital letters | 1 |
| 7 | G6.3: Suffixes | 1 |
| 8 | G1.2: Verbs | 1 |
| 9 | G3.1: Sentences | 1 |
| 10 | G1.3: Adjectives | 1 |
| 11 | G5.4: Exclamation marks | 1 |
| 12 | G2.3: Commands | 1 |
| 13 | G4.1a: Simple past and simple present | 1 |
| 14 | G4.1d: Present and past progressive | 1 |
| 15 | G5.8: Apostrophes | 1 |
| 16 | G4.1a: Simple past and simple present | 2 |
| 17 | G3.2: Noun phrases | 1 |
| 18 | G2.2: Questions | 2 |

## Set B: Grammar, Punctuation and Spelling Paper 2 — Answers

| Qu. | Requirement | Guidance | Marks (Domain) |
|---|---|---|---|
| a | comma | | — (G5.5) |
| b | Answers may vary, for example:<br>• On Thursday, James <u>played</u> football after school.<br>• On Thursday, James <u>coached</u> football after school. | | — (G4.1a) |
| 1 | Yesterday we went to the beach I built a sandcastle.<br>(insert mark ↑ ✓) | | 1 (G5.2) |
| 2 | that | | 1 (G3.4) |
| 3 | ? | Award 1 mark for a question mark at the end of the sentence. | 1 (G5.3) |
| 4 | *vase* and *shelf* | Award 1 mark for both correct. | 1 (G1.1) |
| 5 | adverb | | 1 (G1.6) |
| 6 | *my, jane* and *I* | Award 1 mark for all 3 correct. | 1 (G5.1) |
| 7 | ly | The suffix must be spelt correctly. | 1 (G6.3) |

| Qu. | Requirement | Guidance | Marks (Domain) |
|---|---|---|---|
| 8 | *finished* and *tidied* | Award 1 mark for both correct. | 1 (G1.2) |
| 9 | *He swam 5 km for charity.* | | 1 (G3.1) |
| 10 | *adjective* | | 1 (G1.3) |
| 11 | *exclamation mark* | | 1 (G5.4) |
| 12 | *commands* | | 1 (G2.3) |
| 13 | *gave* | | 1 (G4.1a) |
| 14 | <table><tr><th>Sentence</th><th>Present tense</th><th>Past tense</th></tr><tr><td>She is skipping in the park.</td><td>✓</td><td></td></tr><tr><td>Azmin was singing.</td><td></td><td>✓</td></tr><tr><td>I am cooking dinner.</td><td>✓</td><td></td></tr></table> | Award 1 mark for all 3 correct. | 1 (G4.1d) |
| 15 | *wasn't* | Answer must be spelt correctly. | 1 (G5.8) |
| 16 | *played, was playing* or *had played*<br>*came, were coming* or *had come* | Award 1 mark for each correct answer.<br>Answers must be spelt correctly. | 2 (G4.1a) |
| 17 | *the large blue house* | | 1 (G3.2) |
| 18 | *Answers may vary, for example:*<br>• *Where is Juliet?*<br>• *Do you know where Juliet is?* | Award 2 marks for an appropriate question that is grammatically correct, with correct use of an initial capital letter and question mark.<br>Award 1 mark for an appropriate question that is grammatically correct, with incorrect use of initial capital letter or question mark.<br>No marks should be deducted for incorrect spelling. | 2 (G2.2) |

# CGP

EHEP13U

www.cgpbooks.co.uk